30 Stories, 30 Virtues.

30 Stories, 30 Virtues

Illustrations by Wilfredo C. Jose

ISBN 978-988-79407-4-6

Spring Publications Ltd.
103 Austin Road, Tsimshatsui, Hong Kong

https://www.spring-books.com
info@spring-books.com

To my parents

Thanks be to God,
who gives you a share in the triumph of Christ,
and through you is spreading
the fragrance of Christ everywhere,
the sweet odour of his knowledge (cf. 2 Cor 2:14-15).

May he teach you to profit by the suffering
that comes across your path.
That you may use it
so it will mellow you,
not harden or embitter,
that it may make you patient,
not irritable,
that it may make you broad in your forgiveness,
not narrow, haughty, or overbearing.

May no one be less good
for having come within your influence;
no one less pure,
less true,
less kind,
less noble
for having been a fellow traveller
in your journey toward eternal life.

As you go your rounds
from one distraction to another,
may you whisper from time to time
a word of love to Him.
May your life be lived in the supernatural,
full of power for good,
and strong in its purpose of holiness.

May God shine through you
that every soul with whom you come in contact
may feel His presence
within your soul.
Let them look up
and no longer see you
but only him,
JESUS!

(My parents, Honorio and Purísima, sent me these lines on
the 21st of June 1997, 10th anniversary of my priesthood.
To them these pages are dedicated. The text was adapted
from 2 Cor 2:14-15; Prayer "Learning Christ"; St. John
Henry Newman; "Radiating Christ"; St. Mother Teresa)

CONTENTS

30 STORIES, 30 VIRTUES
CONTENTS
CHARITY
JUSTICE
1. GOD
2. FAMILY
3. OTHERS
4. WORK
5. SELF

Foreword   x

Be a Lady, or a Gentleman, then Be a Saint   1

First Is First   3

Putting Our Thoughts in Order   6

Where Did My Heart Go?   9

Making Time   12

The Battle against Clutter   15

Holiness Is in the Details   18

The Gift of Friendship   22

Doing the Right Thing at the Right Time   25

On Things that We Like Too Much   29

You Need to Have Guts   32

Giving What Each One Deserves   36

Giving to God What Is God's   39

A Duty Always and Everywhere   43

Think Big   46

Contents

Going the Extra Mile — 50

Learning How to Wait — 53

Going All the Way — 56

Surpass Yourself — 59

Catching God's Attention — 63

In the Presence of the Great "Other" — 66

Not to Be Served but to Serve — 70

Humiliation Can Be Good for You — 73

Inner Peace: Fruit of Humility — 76

On Not Taking Oneself too Seriously — 80

Choosing Joy — 84

The Conversation that Never Happened — 88

He Puts You at Ease — 91

"Slow to Anger" — 95

"They Shall See God" — 99

Foreword

The human virtues constitute the foundation for the supernatural virtues. *The Catechism of the Catholic Church* teaches us that "[h]uman virtues are firm attitudes, stable dispositions, habitual perfections of intellect and will that govern our actions, order our passions, and guide our conduct according to reason and faith. They make possible ease, self-mastery, and joy in leading a morally good life. The virtuous man is he who freely practices the good. The moral virtues are acquired by human effort. They are the fruit and seed of morally good acts; they dispose all the powers of the human being for communion with divine love."

I found an opportunity to distill some of the most important human virtues in a series of articles that appeared in *O Clarim,* Macau's trilingual

Catholic Weekly, from 10 June 2016 to 20 January 2017. I have retained the content of the articles as they were published. Thus, the reader will find constant mention of the article "from last week" or "next week."

I hope that this book can provide some simple tips on how to practice these virtues and encourage the reader to try them out in his everyday life.

01
Be a Lady, or a Gentleman, then Be a Saint

St. John Mary Vianney (1786–1859) was once visited by a nobleman from Paris who, like thousands of others, sought him for confession. After his turn was over, this nobleman approached the assistant parish priest and asked him, "Tell me, which noble family does Father Vianney come from?"

"He comes from a simple peasant family," the assistant parish priest replied.

"Oh, but he treated me with such exquisite refinement, I thought he must come from the nobility!"

St. Paul tells us that our Christian life leads us to attain "mature manhood, to the measure of the stature of the fulness of Christ; so that we may no longer be children, tossed to and fro" (Ephesians 4:13–14).

We are all called to be holy, and holiness requires that we be fully human, just as Jesus was: "perfect God and perfect Man" (*Athanasian Creed*).

And what does it mean to be fully human?

It means developing those qualities which we appreciate in a fellow human being. We call them human virtues. St. Thomas Aquinas defines human virtue as "an operative habit, is a good habit, productive of good works" (*Summa Theologiæ*, I-II q55 a3).

Ask yourself: what qualities would I like to see in the people who live or work with me? Would I want them to be honest or deceitful, hard-working or indolent, orderly or messy, good-natured or mean, loyal or unreliable, gentle or irritable? The good qualities we expect from others (and which we ourselves need to develop) are what we call human virtues.

St. Josemaría once wrote something that struck me: "Remember that your virtue may seem to be that of a saint and yet be worth nothing if it is not joined to the ordinary virtues of a Christian. That would be like adorning yourself with magnificent jewels over your underwear" (*The Way,* no. 409).

St. Luke tells us that Jesus "grew and became strong, filled with wisdom" (2:40), "increased in wisdom and in stature, and in favor with God and man" (2:52)—His human intellect and His human will were formed and shaped under the guidance of our Lady and St. Joseph. They trained Jesus, Son of God, in the human virtues. They brought

Him up as a gentleman.

Jesus calls us to follow Him, to attain "mature manhood, to the measure of the stature of the fulness of Christ" (Ephesians 4:13–14). He tells us, "Be a lady, or a gentleman, then be a saint."

02
First Is First

A young man once asked Blessed Álvaro del Portillo, "Father, I think God is asking something of me, but I think my parents want me to do another thing. What do I do?"

Blessed Álvaro smiled and told him, "The first commandment is first, and the fourth is fourth."

Last week, we saw that holiness requires us to grow in the human virtues, good human qualities that we would like to see in our own family, among our friends and colleagues, and which we ourselves have to cultivate. One of these human virtues is that of order which can be defined simply as *having a sense of priorities:* first is first, fourth is fourth.

People in business understand the importance of this concept because it makes operations efficient and productive.

The Chinese classic *Great Learning* (attributed to Confucius) teaches: "The ancients who wished to illustrate illustrious virtue throughout the kingdom, first ordered well their own *States*. Wishing to order well their States, they first regulated their *families*. Wishing to regulate their families, they first cultivated their *persons*. Wishing to cultivate their persons, they first rectified their *hearts*. Wishing to rectify their hearts, they first sought to be sincere in their *thoughts*. Wishing to be sincere in their thoughts, they first extended to the utmost their *knowledge*. Such extension of knowledge lay in the *investigation of things*."

If order is important in human affairs, it is even more essential to living our faith. If we want to be holy, we have to be orderly, always working with a clear sense of priorities. The book of Genesis tells us that God worked in an orderly, not in a haphazard, way. The book of Wisdom (11:20) prays: "Thou hast arranged all things by measure and number and weight." God asks us to imitate Him in His work, He wants us to imitate Him in His *orderly* work. This is why St. Josemaría says, "Virtue without order? Strange virtue!" (*The Way*, no. 79)

Putting order into our lives, however, is not easy. My Chemistry professor in university would tell us that our class followed the law of entropy. What's that? Simply put, entropy is the measure of disorder within a system. The second law of thermodynamics states that, in an isolated system, entropy (i.e., disorder) tends to increase to the maximum. When a star collapses into a black hole, its entropy has increased enormously. So, what our professor meant is that when she was not around, our class would inevitably descend into disorder. Reversing it required an input of energy.

Putting order into our life, correcting the disorder and chaos within, likewise requires an input of energy, it calls for effort. Pope Benedict XVI once said, "The world offers you comfort. But you were not made for comfort. You were made for greatness."

03
Putting Our Thoughts in Order

It was the first day of school in the fall of 1917 in Logroño, Spain. As the students of Don Rafael Escriche filed into the classroom, a dirty and messy chemistry laboratory greeted them. The teacher, not wishing to waste any moment, instructed the students to take only the test tubes, beakers and flasks that they needed for each class, clean them thoroughly before and after use, then store them neatly in their respective shelves. In this way, after a few classes, every piece of equipment had been cleaned and properly stored. One of his students, St. Josemaría, remembered this practical lesson all his life and applied it whenever he was faced with a similar situation. Later on he would write: "'Great' holiness consists in fulfilling the 'little duties' of each moment" (*The Way,* no. 817).

We have seen previously that God works in an orderly way and he invites us to live an orderly life, with a clear sense of priorities: *God, family, others, work,* then—last of all—*self.* When we disregard this hierarchy (such as when *Facebook* wins over the Rosary, or Disneyland takes the place of Sunday Mass, or a car replaces a third child) we slide into chaos ("entropy"). Sin is basically a breakdown in order—it is a disorder.

There are many aspects of our life where we need to observe order: in our *things,* in our *time,* in our *heart,* in our *thoughts.* But we could say that it all begins with *order in our thoughts.* If my thoughts were in disarray, if my mind were cluttered, my spoken or written words would make little or no sense, my actions would probably be inconsistent or erratic as well. This is why I need to form and discipline my mind.

Thus, the *Great Learning,* part of which we read last week, goes on to say: "*Things* being investigated, knowledge became complete. Their *knowledge* being complete, their *thoughts* were sincere. Their thoughts being sincere, their *hearts* were then rectified. Their hearts being rectified, their *persons* were cultivated. Their persons being cultivated, their *families* were regulated. Their families being regulated, their *States* were rightly governed. Their States being rightly governed, the whole *kingdom* was made tranquil and happy."

What can we do to investigate things, to make our knowledge complete? One important way is by reading worthwhile books. When properly chosen, books broaden our knowledge of reality, they provide fresh insight, they help us organize our ideas in a logical way, they train us in critical thinking. We become like *nanos gigantum humeris insidentes* (Latin for "dwarfs standing on the shoulders of giants"), people who build on the knowledge of wise men of the past.

This is even more important for Catholics. One of the greatest enemies of faith is ignorance. We should have a regular time for daily reading of some spiritual book, say, 10 to 15 minutes each day. Ask your spiritual director for a book that suits you.

You have no spiritual director? Then start scouting for one—right now!

04
Where Did My Heart Go?

It happened in October 1995. Pope John Paul II was going to visit Baltimore and the Vatican's chief organizer of papal journeys, Father Roberto Tucci, SJ, was overseeing the preparations for the trip. He was shown the archbishop's residence, where the Pope would eat and rest for a while.

Along a hallway through which the Holy Father would pass was a door that led to the chapel. Father Tucci instructed them: "Keep that door closed so he doesn't know there's a chapel there." It had happened on previous trips that once he had entered a chapel, John Paul II would pray for a long time and the whole itinerary would be thrown into disarray.

When the day came for the visit, they made sure the chapel door was closed. But on the way out, John Paul II stopped in front of the closed chapel door. Father Michael White, the organizer in Baltimore recounted: "He's never been in this place before, never set eyes on the place, and there was nothing about the door that distinguished it in any way as a chapel. It was just one more door in a corridor of doors. But he turned right back around, he opened that door up, and he went into the chapel and he prayed" (in Jason Evert, *St. John Paul the Great*, p. 138).

St. John Paul II certainly *knew* what was most important, a result of *personal study and prayer* through which he found "the pearl of great price" (Matthew 13:45–46), and he *put his heart* into it, for "where the treasure is, there the heart is" (cf. Matthew 6:21; Luke 12:34). Where my treasure is, there my heart goes. And where my heart goes, there I invest *time*. If something is important for me, I make time for it. Hence, order in my time depends on the order in my heart.

At day's end, when I review what I have done, I can easily discover where my heart is, what is most precious for me. I will know by the time I have dedicated to it or the priority I have given to it. "And what, for you, is the most important, most precious thing, that which attracts your heart like a magnet?" Pope Francis asks.

The saints were and will always be the

greatest lovers of all times, because the one they love is the greatest Treasure of all, the greatest Good we can ever possess.

If I discover that my heart is attracted by something different from God, and I dedicate more quality time to other concerns, I know I have to try and know Him better. *Nihil volitum nisi præcognitum*—Nothing is loved unless it has first been known. I need to go back and investigate, to explore my faith, my friendship with Him. "*Things* being investigated, knowledge became complete. Their *knowledge* being complete, their *thoughts* were sincere. Their thoughts being sincere, their *hearts* were then rectified" (*The Great Learning*).

05
Making Time

It was the early morning of Thursday, May 14, 1981.

The day before, Mehmet Ali Ağca, a gunman from Turkey, had fired several shots at Pope John Paul II during the regular Wednesday audience at St. Peter's Square. Four bullets struck the Pope who, right away, was rushed to the Gemelli Hospital where he was operated on. John Paul II miraculously survived, and was brought to the intensive care unit.

Now in the early hours of dawn, the Pope became fully conscious, looked at Stanisław Dziwisz his personal secretary (now a Cardinal and Archbishop of Kraków), and remarked, "We have not said Complines yet." Complines is the last part of the Liturgy of the Hours and the Pope thought it was still Wednesday.

Dziwisz was impressed at the remark.

There was no comment about pain, about what happened. John Paul II was only concerned about his regular appointment with his Lord.

How different it is with us. We take time for personal things, but as for things related to God, they can wait, they can be postponed, forgotten, cancelled, or rushed.

Take the Mass, for instance. St. Josemaría comments, "Isn't it strange how many Christians, who take their time and have leisure enough in their social life (they are in no hurry), in following the sleepy rhythm of their professional affairs, in eating and recreation (no hurry here either), find themselves rushed and want to rush the Priest, in their anxiety to shorten the time devoted to the most holy Sacrifice of the Altar?" (*The Way,* no. 530).

I once read this story of a man who professed to be a believer, but he had one great defect: he would always postpone things. He was always late for Mass and when the time for helping others or the time of prayer came, many times he would say, "Later."

Finally, he died.

How great was his joy when he found himself outside the gates of heaven, and even more so when St. Peter turned, saw him, and smiled at him.

"Can I go in now?"

"Later," Peter replied.

Jesus told the Samaritan woman: "If you knew the gift of God, and who it is that is saying to you, 'Give me a drink,' you would have asked him, and he would have given you living water" (John 4:10).

If we only *knew* the gifts that the Lord showers on us during prayer and in the sacraments, we would put our *heart* into the things of God. If we put our heart into them, we will *make time* for them.

Let us say that a rich man who lived an hour away from your house decided he would give away $10,000 each day at 5 AM to anyone who asked. Would you get up and go at that early hour? You probably would. Well, every single Mass is infinitely more valuable than millions of dollars.

So if we want to give more time for our Lord, we need to know Him better. That's why we need to read more about Him.

By the way, have you asked your spiritual director about what spiritual reading book suits you?

06
The Battle against Clutter

This report from *Reuters* came just one week ago:

"Fumio Sasaki's one-room Tokyo apartment is so stark friends liken it to an interrogation room. He owns three shirts, four pairs of trousers, four pairs of socks and a meager scattering of various other items.

"Money isn't the issue. The 36-year-old editor has made a conscious lifestyle choice, joining a growing number of Japanese deciding that less is more."

Sasaki's lifestyle contrasts with the great majority of us who are overwhelmed with clutter.

For some people, clutter can be the result of compulsive hoarding or impulsive buying, a kind of "I-might-need-this-later" mentality, or a sentimental attachment to things.

For others it can be result of procrastination, putting things off for later. One time management expert says that "at bottom, each item of clutter is a decision delayed" (Cynthia Ewer).

There can be many reasons for putting off a decision. Sometimes, it is prudence. Sometimes it can be fear, or perhaps, laziness.

"'To-morrow': sometimes it is prudence; very often it is the adverb of the defeated" (St. Josemaría, *The Way,* no. 251).

St. Josemaría loved to repeat two Latin words: *"hodie et nunc"* — today and now. He argued that the only real thing is the present moment, the NOW. The past is gone, and the future is yet to come.

We sometimes fool ourselves into thinking that time is ours, that we possess it. In fact, what we have is only one moment: **this present moment**. "Therefore do not be anxious about tomorrow, for tomorrow will be anxious for itself. Let the day's own trouble be sufficient for the day" (Matthew 6:34). God made us for greatness, but that greatness is composed of every present moment lived to the full. God invites us to focus on each moment and give it our best shot. In this way we avoid clutter and chaos.

Each one of us will have to find a way to organize ourselves. One organizational expert suggests a way of dealing with office work.

"Only Handle it Once simply means that

each time you handle a piece of paper you should take the NEXT step necessary to finish dealing with it. Once the paper has been dealt with, it can be filed (if you need/want to keep it), tossed, recycled or shredded (if you don't) or given to someone else for further action.

"Picking up a piece of paper and putting it back down **without taking action** is a waste of time, so DON'T do it."

And how do we avoid accumulating things we don't need? One way is by asking oneself: will I really use this in the next 12 months? On what occasion? If the answer is No, then we should forget about buying or keeping it.

Keeping clutter out of our life is a daily struggle for all of us. Put more positively, it is the struggle to restore order, not only in our things or our time, but also in our minds and hearts.

It is a struggle that must begin today and now.

07
Holiness Is in the Details

"Simon, I have something to tell you," the Lord told the Pharisee who had invited him (Luke 7:40).

"What is it, Teacher?" Simon replied.

Then Jesus began to point out details that Simon, a respectable man, had missed out: "You gave me no water for my feet.... You gave me no kiss.... You did not anoint my head with oil..." (Luke 7:44, 45, 46). Foot-washing (especially for guests coming from a journey) and kissing were customs of courtesy. The anointing of the head was a sign of deference. Simon had neglected all these.

"Jesus notices the omission of the expression of human courtesy and refinement which the Pharisee failed to show him," St. Josemaría Escrivá writes in *Friends of God*.

To be holy, one needs to learn how to be a lady or a gentleman. Being a lady or a gentleman means paying attention to little things and tiny details.

"Don't despise little things, for by the continual practice of denying yourself again and again in such things—which are never futile or trivial—with God's grace you will add strength and resilience to your character. In that way you will first become master of yourself, and then a guide, a chief, a leader: to compel and to urge and to inspire others, with your word, with your example, with your knowledge and with your power" (St. Josemaría, *The Way,* no 19).

As Lau Bei (劉備) of the *Three Kingdoms* told his only son: "Do not fail to do a good act just because it is small in scale. Do not commit evil even if it seems insignificant."

Linda Kaplan Thaler and Robin Koval, in their book *The Power of Small: Why Little Things Make All the Difference,* say that "if we can't take care of the small details, how can we be counted on to deliver when it really matters?" They argue that we need to pay attention to "small details that, if disregarded, can sabotage a multimillion-dollar ad campaign or undermine your most important relationships."

That's not really new, is it? More than 2000 years ago, Jesus not only praised but **promised**

heaven to the man who is faithful in little things. "Well done, good and faithful servant; you have been faithful over a little, I will set you over much; enter into the joy of your master" (Matthew 25:23).

If little details are important for earthly affairs, then they also play an even bigger role in the spiritual life.

"Do you really want to be a saint? Carry out the little duty of each moment: do what you ought and concentrate on what you are doing" (*The Way,* no. 815).

Where do we find these little details? Everywhere. At home, at work, in the kitchen, out in the street, in the ballcourt, in the supermarket, on the bus, in church.

Pope Francis has often encouraged us to use those little phrases that build a home: "Please" or "May I," "Sorry," "Thank you." Indeed, these simple phrases are useful on all occasions.

And whether it be at home, at work, or in our social relations, we all know there is a world of difference between a little sneer and a little smile. It takes effort to control a moment of impatience, but its long-term benefits are ours to enjoy. A Chinese maxim goes: "If one can endure for a moment, one will not be worried for a hundred days."

Technology has made it possible for us to do things more efficiently. But it is no excuse for not taking time to compose and check the emails we send. When I was working on my thesis, I was impressed by the emails I received from my thesis adviser (he has several books to his name in several languages). Each one was not only positive and encouraging, he made sure there were no typographical mistakes and he even indented the paragraphs!

When taking meals at home or in a restaurant, it takes just a moment to say grace before and after meals. But it could be our daily contribution to the new evangelization. We may not have a chance to preach to crowds, but we have shown what faith is.

When there is love, especially love for God, one notices the details. "Great souls pay much attention to little things" (*The Way,* no. 818).

By keeping an eye on the little details in our life, we advance slowly, surely towards holiness. It does not matter how slow we go. But what counts is that we take one little step each time. As the Chinese saying goes, be not afraid to go slow, but be afraid of stopping.

08
The Gift of Friendship

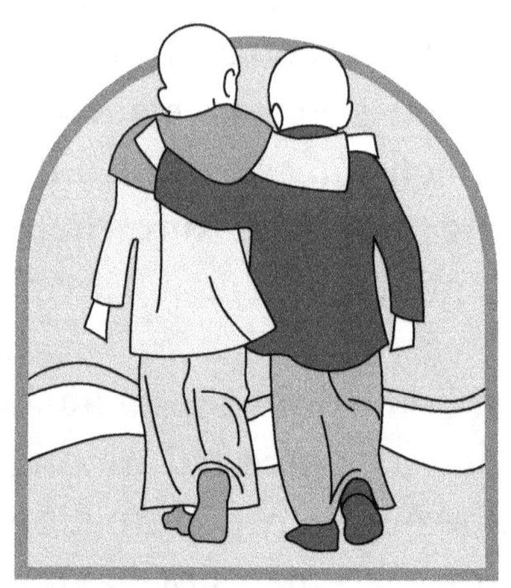

In June 1984, Pope John Paul II sent his personal secretary Stanisław Dziwisz with three other Polish priests to scout around for a place where they could ski. Once they had found an ideal spot in the Italian Alps, they started organizing the first papal skiing excursion.

But, of course, the Pope would need to fly there, and to do that, the Vatican had to ask the Italian Air Force for a helicopter. And word soon got to the Italian President—at the time it was Sandro Pertini—about the request. Though a Socialist, he was a very good friend of the Holy Father. He could not control his curiosity about why the Pope would go to a place far away from the crowds. So he personally rang up the Pope to inquire.

The Pope replied, "I'm going skiing. Why don't you come, too?"

So that was how the 88-year-old Italian President joined his friend in an excursion to the Alps.

Friendship is not only human. It is divine. Jesus told His apostles, "I have called you friends!" (John 15:15).

St. Josemaría says that the apostolate of ordinary Christians is an apostolate of friendship and trust.

What does it take to be a friend? Here are some ingredients.

1. **Respect.** We have to respect our friend because he, like us, is endowed with freedom and the consequent responsibility, and hence the capacity for self-determination. Besides, each one is a child of God, and God has a master plan for each one. Friendship "means rejoicing at their road to God" (St. Josemaría, *Furrow,* no. 757).

2. **Thoughtfulness.** A thoughtful person spends more time thinking about what he can do for others than what they can do for him.

3. **Kindness.** "It's not enough to be good; you need to show it" (St. Josemaría, *Furrow,* no. 735). A little kindness goes a long way. Kindness attracts, harshness repels.

4. **Considerateness and tact.** "Your charity must be adapted and tailored to the needs of others,

not to yours" (St. Josemaría, *Furrow,* no. 749).

5. **A ready and attentive ear.** Knowing how to let the other person speak, learning to listen even to things that are not said, knowing how to watch out for nuances, will also help us build a friendship.

6. **Understanding.** No one's perfect. Each one has his share of defects. Mother Teresa says, "If you judge people, you have no time to love them."

7. **Appreciation** and **gratitude.** Nothing is more encouraging and motivates a person than honest praise, nothing more uplifting than a word of thanks.

8. **Loyalty.** "A friend loves at all times" (Proverbs 17:17).

9. **Sincerity.** St. Thomas Aquinas teaches: "Nevertheless, as the Philosopher [Aristotle] says, for the sake of some good that will result, or in order to avoid some evil, the virtuous man will sometimes not shrink from bringing sorrow to those among whom he lives. Hence the Apostle says (II Corinthians 7:8): 'Although I made you sorrowful by my epistle, I do not repent,' and further on (II Corinthians 7:9), 'I am glad; not because you were made sorrowful, but because you were made sorrowful unto repentance'" (*Summa Theologiæ* II-II q 114, a 1, ad3).

10. **Patience.** It takes time to learn. It takes

time to mature. "Behold, the farmer waits for the precious fruit of the earth, being patient over it until it receives the early and the late rain. You also be patient. ... Do not grumble, brethren, against one another, that you may not be judged" (James 5:7-9). St. Josemaría would often say, "Good souls, like wine, improve with time."

09
Doing the Right Thing at the Right Time

Ravi Shankar, founder of the Art of Living Foundation, narrates that once, "Mahatma Gandhi was travelling in a small train uphill to Darjeeling. Darjeeling is a hill station in India.... When the train was moving up the hill, somewhere, the engine got itself disconnected from the coaches. So the engine went ahead and the coaches started sliding backward.

"There was huge panic, as people were between life and death. Any moment the coaches could fall off the hill.... It was the Himalayas.

"So while there was panic all around, Mahatma Gandhi was dictating letters, and he said to my teacher; he used to call him Bangalori, because he was from Bangalore; 'Bangalori, take dictation.'

"My teacher said, '*Bapu* ("father," referring to Mahatma Gandhi), do you know what is happening? We may not be alive. We are in-between life and death. The coaches are moving backward with nothing to stop it, and it's gaining speed.'

"[Gandhi] said, 'If we die, we die. But if we are saved, we would have wasted all this time. So, come on, take dictation.'"

The story is clearly about good use of time, but it also points to another virtue, a virtue that helps us to decide on the right thing to do in a particular situation. This virtue is called "**prudence**" (Greek: φρόνησις, *phronēsis;* Latin: *prudentia*).

Prudence is one of the **four cardinal virtues**. The word "cardinal" comes from Latin which means "hinge." The reason they are called "cardinal" is that the moral life hinges on them, in the same way that a door depends on its hinges. The other three are fortitude, justice, and temperance. We can probably call them **key virtues of the moral life**.

The Old Testament speaks about them: "And if any one loves righteousness, her labors are virtues; for she teaches **self-control** and **prudence**, **justice** and **courage**; nothing in life is more profitable for men than these" (Wisdom 8:7).

Plato also spoke about them in the *Republic*. In their own times Aristotle, Cicero, St. Ambrose, St. Augustine, and St. Thomas Aquinas spoke about the cardinal virtues as well.

St. Thomas defines prudence simply as "**right reason applied to action**" (*Summa Theologiæ*, II-IIae, q 47, a 8). Gandhi's argument was definitely right reasoning, he was following correct logic, and he carried it out. He was prudent.

We could probably equate prudence with one of the Five Constant Virtues (五 常): wisdom (智). Indeed, it is also called "wisdom."

Prudence is needed by anyone who has to make decisions, which means all of us. But it is even more needed by one who has authority, because his every decision affects many others. When we lack prudence, we become impetuous, thoughtless, negligent and inconstant.

What characteristics can we find in a prudent man?

1. A prudent man knows the **moral principles** relevant to the situation. Prudence requires formation of one's conscience.

2. He also takes into account the **past**, which includes the experience of other people. He should be eager to learn from others, being ready to listen and to be open-minded. This makes him receptive to the advice and counsel of other people, especially those who are older, more experienced, and more knowledgeable.

3. He has a clear knowledge of the **present** situation. This includes observing and asking the opinion of others, especially those who will be affected by his decision. He should realize that he has his own biases, and he should take these into account when assessing the situation.

4. He considers the different **means** he can use taking into account the advantages and disadvantages, the good points and weak points of each one, and their **future consequences**.

5. Finally, he **makes up his mind**, he **decides** and **acts** on his decision. Many people think prudence only means refraining from action. In many cases, it is the opposite: prudence requires us to act.

10
On Things that We Like Too Much

In 1994, *Time* magazine chose Pope John Paul II as "Man of the Year." On the day that the magazine hit the newsstands, his spokesman quickly got a copy and brought it to the Pope.

Once he was in the Pope's study, he handed the Holy Father the magazine with a contented smile. The Holy Father looked at it, then put it down on his table, with the front cover facing downwards.

"What's wrong, Holy Father, you don't like it?" the spokesman worriedly asked.

"No. The problem is...I like it too much!" he replied.

Last week we spoke about prudence. Prudence is called the *auriga virtutum*, the charioteer of the virtues. The reason for this is that prudence regulates the other virtues, it sets the right measure we need to follow, because we sin either by excess or defect.

Today we talk about **temperance** (Greek: σωφροσύνη, *sōphrosynē;* Latin: *temperantia*). It is the virtue that helps us become masters of things that please us, things we enjoy, things that we "like too much." We need this virtue because there is a danger of overindulging in the things we enjoy, of not following right reason, of letting our feelings rule us, of becoming slaves of our passions, and of not obeying the voice of prudence. When that happens, we fall into excesses like gluttony, drunkenness, and impurity.

Blessed Álvaro del Portillo, commenting on the creation of our first parents, said that God forbade Adam and Eve from eating of the fruit of "the tree of the knowledge of good and evil" (Genesis 2:17) not because the tree itself was bad. Indeed, we know that everything that God made was good. But he forbade them to eat of the fruit of the tree in order to test their obedience.

Blessed Álvaro likewise adds that it is good for us now and then to abstain from a certain good thing—our own "tree of the knowledge of good and evil," that thing that we "like too much"—for the sake of giving glory to God. St. Josemaría suggested a very simple exercise of temperance: to eat less of what we like and eat more of what we don't like.

Moreover, when we practice temperance and offer the sacrifice to God, we are doing **mortification**. Mortification does not only mean fasting. Whenever we exercise self-control, we are practicing mortification.

Other virtues revolve around temperance. Among them are: **continence** which moderates our use of the **sense of touch**; **meekness** which tames **anger**; **clemency** which moves one in authority to reduce or even remit **due punishment** insofar as this is reasonable; **modesty** which regulates external **physical movements** and **appearance**; **moderation** in the use of **material things**; and **humility** which moderates the **desire for self-excellence**. Humility is the foundation of all other virtues, just as its contrary vice, pride, is the root of all sins. Judging by this list, we can understand why temperance is so important for a person to live an upright moral life.

There is an even more important reason. Temperance prepares us to savor the higher things in life, spiritual goods, which are far more lasting and satisfying than earthly pleasures.

The saints seemed like fools because they did not give much importance to earthly power, pleasures, and possessions. But the Last Judgment will show that they have been the wisest, because they had discovered the happiness that is "out of this world."

St. Teresa of Avila exclaimed, *"Oh cuán poco lo de acá, oh cuán mucho lo de allá!"* — How little we have here [on earth], and how much they have there [in heaven]!

Certainly there are plenty of things to enjoy on earth. But all those are only "sneak previews" of what is to come. We enjoy created things, but we were created for far greater joys.

11
You Need to Have Guts

"Why do you think we haven't had a woman as president yet?" First Lady Hillary Rodham Clinton asked her guest over their lunch at the White House.

The little woman sitting at table with Mrs. Clinton did not hesitate in her reply.

"Because she has probably been aborted," said Mother Teresa. (Thanks to Sean Fitzpatrick of *Crisis* Magazine who passed on this story.)

That was not the only time Hillary had met Mother Teresa.

In 1994, Blessed Mother Teresa was invited to speak before the National Prayer Breakfast.

The National Prayer Breakfast is a yearly event held in Washington, DC, on the first Thursday of February each year since 1953. *Wikipedia* says that it is meant to be "a forum for the political, social, and business elite to assemble and build relationships." Hence, it is understandable that speakers are careful not to offend anyone and tend to use the most politically correct discourse.

But Mother Teresa was different. In a speech that was interrupted several times by standing ovation, she spoke clearly and unequivocally.

"But I feel that the greatest destroyer of peace today is abortion, because it is a war against the child, a direct killing of the innocent child, murder by the mother herself.

"And if we accept that a mother can kill even her own child, how can we tell other people not to kill one another?"

She added, "Please don't kill the child. I want the child. Please give me the child. I am willing to accept any child who would be aborted and to give that child to a married couple who will love the child and be loved by the child."

President and Mrs. Clinton were there. They did not stand. They did not applaud. But Mother Teresa spoke on anyway, "with gentleness and reverence" (I Peter 3:15).

As Christians, we need to have guts. In theological language, this is called **fortitude** (Greek: $\dot{\alpha}\nu\delta\rho\varepsilon\dot{\iota}\alpha$, *andreia;* Latin: *fortitudo*). "In the world you have tribulation; but be of good cheer, I have overcome the world" (John 16:33).

If **temperance** helps us to be masters of **things we like, fortitude** helps us face **things we dislike**.

Fortitude involves two things: the **capacity to endure** a difficulty and the **courage to act** to overcome hardship. The first is **passive**, the second **active**.

Just like all other virtues, it is governed by **prudence** and right reason enlightened by faith. For example, putting one's fingers over a flame to see how long one can take the pain is not fortitude. But being tortured for the sake of one's faith is.

Virtues related to fortitude include **magnanimity**, **generosity**, **patience**, **constancy**, and **perseverance**. Here we could also include

meekness—moderating our anger—which (as we have seen) is also related to temperance.

How can ordinary Christians practice fortitude?

We exercise the passive aspect of fortitude when we try to bear cheerfully the little annoyances of daily life. "Many who would willingly let themselves be nailed to a Cross before the astonished gaze of a thousand onlookers cannot bear with a Christian spirit the pinpricks of each day! Think, then, which is the more heroic" (St. Josemaría, *The Way*, no. 204).

We exercise the active aspect of fortitude when we give our very best in every little job and responsibility, in order to give glory to God and to serve others.

The human virtue of fortitude is further strengthened by grace. This is why we have to pray for fortitude and frequently meditate on the Passion of Jesus, who showed us that love makes us strong.

When one has love, one has guts.

12
Giving What Each One Deserves

There once was an old man who lived with the family of one of his married children. As he grew older, he became clumsier. Whenever he ate, he would spill his food. So the family had him eat alone. When he dropped his bowl and broke it, they scolded him and got him a cheap wooden bowl.

One day the young grandson took some wood and started working on it.

"What are you doing?" his Mom and Dad asked.

"I'm making a wooden bowl," he said, "for when you two get old and must eat alone."

The couple realized their mistake and from that time on, they let the old man eat with the family.

We all understand the importance of fairness and justice. You and I, at some moments in our life, will inevitably suffer some form of injustice or discrimination, and we know how it hurts. Jesus suffered the highest form of injustice, because he was absolutely and completely innocent. Unlike us, sinners.

The need for justice arises because man does not live alone—he lives in a society, he interacts with other people. We need a virtue that regulates this interaction.

What is justice? Following St. Thomas Aquinas' definition, the *Catechism of the Catholic Church* teaches: "Justice is the moral virtue that consists in the constant and firm will to give their due to God and neighbor. Justice toward God is called the 'virtue of religion'" (no. 1807).

Justice requires the exercise of the will. This is why it prepares us to practice charity, because charity requires a strong will. Out of justice, we give our neighbor what is his; out of charity, we give what is ours.

Charity is superior to justice, but because justice is more basic than charity, the duties of justice are stricter than those of charity. I cannot love my dad or mom if I do not give them due respect. I cannot say I love God if I don't go to Mass on Sunday (a requirement of justice).

On the other hand, justice alone does not suffice. Justice alone can lead to unjust situations as well. Fr. Paul A. Duffner, O.P., writes "In the settlement of disputes, while justice may accomplish the restoration of rights, it will not of itself restore peace. In this regard St. Thomas Aquinas states: 'Peace is the work of justice indirectly, insofar as it removes the obstacles to peace; but it is the work of charity directly, since charity, according to its very nature causes peace; for love is a unitive force....'"

We Christians must indeed fight for social justice, but justice is not enough. We should aim for higher things, for "a still more excellent way" (I Corinthians 12:31). We should strive to practice charity at home, at work, in society at large. "For I tell you, unless your righteousness exceeds that of the scribes and Pharisees, you will never enter the kingdom of heaven" (Matthew 5:20).

13
Giving to God What Is God's

In 1980, St. John Paul II expressed his desire to bring the Corpus Christi procession back to the streets of Rome. It had been banned in 1870 after the loss of the Papal States. In 1982, he carried out his resolution, personally carrying the monstrance from St. John Lateran to St. Mary Major, a distance.

In later years, when illness weakened the Pope, the Blessed Sacrament was placed on a pedestal and mounted on a special truck, which also had a seat and a kneeler for the Pope. Despite his frailty, the Holy Father always insisted on kneeling, even when he was quite weak, saying: "My Lord is there!"

Last week we spoke about justice, about giving others what they have a right to. Well, the most important "Other" is God. Giving him what He has a right to is called the virtue of **religion**.

To practice this virtue is to practice justice in its highest form.

We are sometimes very eager to claim our rights but can be neglectful in doing our duties. This is especially true in our relationship with God. We demand that He listen, that He pay attention, that He reply quickly, that He grant what we ask or that He explain why He does not grant us what we ask, and many of us can't even make it to 1 hour of Sunday Mass despite the 168 hours He gives us each week! And we say God is unfair.

What does the virtue of religion require of us? For all Christians, it demands **adoration, prayer, sacrifice,** and **offering**. For religious and married people, **vows**.

Let's talk a bit about adoration.

The devil does not want us to adore God. He would rather we adore ourselves: "You will be like God" (Genesis 3:5), he told our first parents. He said this not because he thinks man is worthy of adoration. Not at all. He knows that once we stop adoring God, we cut ourselves off from the source of everything that is true, good, beautiful, and adorable in our lives. Man is God's image. Once God is gone, his image disappears as well. Man loses his dignity and can then be easily used and manipulated.

On the other hand, a person who adores becomes a force for good in the world. Pope Francis once remarked, "Think of Mother Teresa: what does the spirit of the world say of Mother Teresa? 'Ah, Blessed Teresa is a beautiful woman, she did a lot of good things for others …'. The spirit of the world never says that the Blessed Teresa spent, every day, many hours, in adoration…never! It reduces Christian activity to doing social good" (Homily, May 28, 2013).

During the preparations for the Conclave that elected Pope Francis, the future Pope (Cardinal Jorge Mario Bergoglio) spoke to the cardinals saying, "Thinking of the next Pope: He must be a man who, from the contemplation and adoration of Jesus Christ, helps the Church to go out to the existential peripheries, that helps her to be the fruitful mother, who gains life from 'the sweet and comforting joy of evangelizing.'"

Whether it be helping the poorest of the poor or being Roman Pontiff, everything must always start from adoration.

Adoration requires the participation of the **whole person**, of **both soul and body**. **Interiorly**, we need to humble ourselves before the One Who created us, Who redeemed us, and Who sanctifies us. **Exteriorly**, we bend our knees before Him Who is our Beginning, our End, our

Life, our All.

We adore especially at Mass, the highest form of adoration. But we can and should also adore anywhere and anytime. Indeed, as St. Josemaría taught, anything we do can be turned not only into **adoration**, but can also be turned into **prayer**, into a **sacrifice**, and into an **offering**. Every single act we do can be a four-in-one package! How?

"Whether you eat or drink, or whatever you do, **do all to the glory of God**" (I Corinthians 10:31). A policeman directing traffic, a teacher imparting a lesson, a mother giving milk to her baby, a farmer plowing the field, an airline pilot taking a plane into the air, a student preparing an exam: they all can turn everything into adoration, prayer, sacrifice, offering. Work becomes an occasion for giving God what belongs to God.

14
A Duty Always and Everywhere

It was a charming sight. The little girl had approached the ticket vending machine inside the Taipei MRT station. Following all the verbal instructions, she managed to make the purchase and when the machine told her that the ticket was ready, she reached for it, took a bow before the machine, and said, *"Xie xie!"* — "Thank you!"

Part of good upbringing is learning how to say thank you. Our parents made sure we acquired the habit.

To acknowledge a favor, a person's goodwill, or a gift, is a duty of justice. It is part of good manners. The person who has received a gift or been done a favor needs to recognize what the other has done for him. And, as we have seen, the most important "Other" is God.

Whenever Jesus prayed, he always started with a thank you to God the Father. The

Catechism of the Catholic Church (no. 2604) recalls, for instance, the fact that Jesus, before raising Lazarus, prayed thus: "Father, I thank you for having heard me." Jesus did this all the time. Thanked the Father first. Always.

When we are at Mass, the celebrant says on our behalf: "It is truly right and just, our duty and our salvation always and everywhere to give you thanks, Lord, holy Father..." Always, everywhere. Do I do that?

And why always, why everywhere? Because God is always blessing me. He blesses me with things I call "good" and things I call "bad"—he blesses me with His cross, honors me with it.

When we ask a priest for blessing he makes the sign of the Cross. God blesses us in many ways, and one of those ways is through the cross. The cross purifies us, strengthens us, gives us a chance to participate in saving souls.

Again, the *Catechism* (no. 2648) teaches us: "Every joy and suffering, every event and need can become the matter for thanksgiving which, sharing in that of Christ, should fill one's whole life: 'Give thanks in all circumstances' (1 Thessalonians 5:18)."

St. Josemaría once said that when we are able to thank God for everything that happens to us, we have advanced a great deal in the spiritual life. Many times during the day, he would repeat a prayer of thanksgiving: "I give you thanks, almighty God, for all your benefits, *etiam ignotis*—including those I am not aware of or which I ignore...."

God keeps on blessing us, but we easily take his blessings for granted. "Sometimes those whom Jesus has called to be His close friends, those upon whom He has bestowed a privileged vocation, are the very ones who show Him the least gratitude" (Fr. Gabriel of St. Mary Magdalene, *Divine Intimacy* 283, 1).

Let us learn to say thank you, again and again. St. Teresa of Avila exclaimed: "Oh! How the very greatness of His favors condemns those who are ungrateful!"

Gratitude attracts more grace. It makes our prayers more effective. Our own experience tells us that it is easier to do favors for those who know how to recognize what we do for them than for those who take our goodwill for granted.

Gratitude makes us discover things to be thankful for. When we start thanking God, we realize that He is blessing us in so many ways all the time.

Gratitude helps us to be humble, and reminds us that we depend on others for so many things.

Heavenly Father, I thank You "for all You

have given, for all You have withheld, for all You have withdrawn, for all You have permitted, for all You have prevented; for all You have forgiven me, for all You have prepared for me, for the death You have chosen for me, for the place You are keeping for me in heaven, for having created me to love You for all eternity." Thank You, thank You, thank You! (Litany of Thanksgiving).

15
Think Big

In 1921, an unknown surgeon named Frederick Banting with a bachelor's degree in medicine thought of a way to extract the substance that could cure diabetes. Banting proposed the idea to the leading figure in the study of diabetes in Canada at the time, Professor John Macleod. Macleod did not give much importance to Banting's theories, but Banting managed to convince Macleod to give him a laboratory with a minimum of equipment. Banting also got an assistant, a medical student by the name of Charles Best.

So the two set to work. In January 1922, the substance called "insulin" was first tested on a diabetic 14-year-old boy, Leonard Thompson. It was a success.

In 1923, Banting and Macleod won the Nobel Prize in Medicine. Banting, who thought that his assistant Dr. Charles Best deserved more, shared the award money with him.

Large pharmaceutical companies offered Banting huge sums of money for the patent to insulin. They proposed to put Banting in charge of an insulin clinic, and would make the medicine available to all who could pay for it.

Banting, however, said that insulin was his gift to mankind, and it would be available to everyone who needed it rather than a commodity for anyone's profit.

Great man, great heart, great soul: an example of magnanimity.

"Magnanimity" comes from the Latin roots *magna*, great, and *animus*, mind. The *Catholic Encyclopedia* (Revised Edition by Our Sunday Visitor) defines it as the "virtue which prompts one to do morally good acts of exceptional quality. Magnanimous persons are disposed to perform actions of extraordinary generosity, kindness, fortitude and charity; not in order to gain fame, glory or recognition, but simply to do what is right, good, just or needed."

Magnanimity is a characteristic of saints. Saints think big.

Noah Webster describes magnanimity as "greatness of mind; that elevation or dignity of soul, which encounters danger and trouble with tranquility and firmness, which raises the possessor above revenge, and makes him delight in acts of benevolence, which makes him disdain injustice and meanness, and prompts him to sacrifice personal ease, interest and safety for the accomplishment of useful and noble objects."

Magnanimity stands in the middle between pusillanimity on one hand, and presumption, vainglory, ambition on the other.

Pusillanimity (literally "smallness of soul") is narrow-mindedness, meanness. The pusillanimous man is constantly thinking about himself and not able to face the sacrifice of giving himself to others. He lives in a very small world—his own tiny comfortable world. He does not aim very high. He wallows in mediocrity, he has "opted for early retirement," according to Pope Francis.

On the other hand, we become **presumptuous** when we think we can do more than what we are really capable of. The book of Revelation has very strong words for the presumptuous: "you say, I am rich, I have prospered, and I need nothing; not knowing that you are wretched, pitiable, poor, blind, and naked" (3:17).

We are **vain** when we want others to think well of us, to talk well about us, to listen to us, to ask for our opinion, to admire us and praise us. We are vain when we think we are the center of attention. And when it seems that others are not paying attention to us, we try to do anything to call their attention.

The magnanimous man dreams big, but not for his own sake. There is a good kind of **ambition**, and a bad kind. Indeed, the saints were the most ambitious persons who ever lived. They were ambitious out of love for God.

But the bad kind of ambition comes from pride. It only desires personal excellence as suggested by the serpent: "You will be like God" (Genesis 3:5).

16
Going the Extra Mile

"And if anyone forces you to go one mile, go with him two miles" (Matthew 5:41).

George C. Boldt was a poor immigrant from central Europe and had come to New York in the 1860s. He first worked as a dishwasher at the Merchants' Exchange Hotel, then went to Texas to look for a better job but could not find one. He went back to New York and took another kitchen job and was promoted to a cashier position. A New York hotel owner was impressed by his industriousness and attention to service and decided to offer him a position as a hotel manager. In that position, Boldt turned a 24-room hotel on Philadelphia's Broad Street into the Bellevue, the best hotel in Philadelphia.

One rainy night, a man and his wife came looking for a room. That night, however, all the rooms in the Bellevue were booked. Boldt, however, did not want to send them away and instead offered them his own room. They were hesitant at first, but Boldt convinced them to take his offer.

The man who took Boldt's room with his wife happened to be millionaire William Waldorf Astor. A short time later, he built the Waldorf Hotel in the site of his old mansion in New York. Its first manager? George C. Boldt. It was Boldt who established the exquisite level of service for which the Waldorf (later called the Waldorf-Astoria) has become world famous. And it all started with one act of generosity, when one man's service went the extra mile.

Wikipedia defines generosity as "the virtue of not being tied down by concerns about one's possessions. Often it means to provide help to others by giving them an (usually precious) item without thinking twice." Generosity is the habit of giving freely—money, possessions, time, attention, assistance, encouragement, a smile, emotional availability—without expecting anything in return.

Philosophy Professor Donald DeMarco says, "In gratitude we are human; in generosity we are divine: 'You received without pay, give without pay'" (Matthew 10:8).

One day, a ten-year-old boy went to an ice cream shop, sat at a table and asked the waitress,

"How much is an ice cream cone?"

She said, "75 cents."

The boy started counting the coins he had in his hand. Then he asked how much a small cup of ice cream was.

The waitress impatiently replied, "65 cents."

The boy said, "I will have the small ice cream cup."

He had his ice cream, paid the bill and left. When the waitress came to pick up the empty plate, she was touched. Underneath were ten cents as tip.

Generosity is infectious, it inspires others to be generous as well.

Generosity spawns gratitude, gladdens the heart, generates hope.

Among the gifts that we can give, the most valuable one is the gift of ourselves. The best example of that self-giving is Jesus Christ. No one can match His generosity in giving, and in rewarding.

"Receive, O Lord, all my liberty. Take my memory, my understanding, and my entire will. Whatsoever I have or hold, You have given me; I give it all back to You and surrender it wholly to be governed by Your will. Give me only Your love and Your grace, and I am rich enough and ask for nothing more" (St. Ignatius of Loyola).

17
Learning How to Wait

Aman observed a woman in the grocery store with a three-year- old girl in her shopping cart.

As they passed the cookie section, the little girl asked for cookies and her mother told her no. The little girl immediately began to whine and fuss.

The mother said quietly, "Now Monica, we just have half of the aisles left to go through; don't be upset. It won't be long."

Soon they came to the candy aisle, and the little girl began to shout for candy. And when told she couldn't have any, began to cry.

The mother said, "There, there, Monica, only two more aisles to go, and then we'll be checking out."

When they got to the checkout stand, the little girl immediately began to clamor for gum and burst into a terrible tantrum upon discovering there would be no gum purchased.

The mother patiently said, "Monica, we'll be through this check out stand in 5 minutes and then you can go home and have a nice nap."

The man followed them out to the parking lot and stopped the woman to compliment her.

"I couldn't help noticing how patient you were with little Monica," he said.

The mother chuckled and said, "I'm Monica... my little girl's name is Tammy."

All our life we have to learn many things, and one of them is to wait, to be patient. Just how important is it? Jesus says, "By your patience you will win your souls" (Luke 21:19).

Everyone needs to learn how to be patient. A wife needs to be patient with her husband, and a husband with his wife. Parents need to be patient with their children and children need to be patient with their parents. Siblings have to be patient with one another. Priests need to be patient with their faithful and the faithful with their priests. Teachers need to be patient with their students and students with their teachers. Superiors need to be patient with their subordinates and subordinates with their superiors. Co-workers, acquaintances, friends have to be patient with one another. And so on.

Moreover, we have also to be patient when

circumstances are adverse, such as when the weather is unpleasant or when things don't turn out the way we planned. "Patience helps one to encounter frustrations, disappointments, contradictions, privations, sickness, hardships, etc., (all of which cause pain) without losing his serenity, without becoming irritated or despondent. It helps one not to be upset by trivial incidents however unpleasant in our daily lives and thus not lose peace of soul" (Fr. Paul A. Duffner, O.P.).

But what do we do with the pain? We offer it to God, the way Jesus offered His sufferings to the Father. In that way, we not only bear pain, but we "sanctify pain" (St. Josemaría).

Does it mean that we should be merely passive when we encounter injustice? Not at all. Cowardice is not patience. When a situation harms others, the common good, and especially God's honor, we should act decisively (as much as possible with charity) to correct the wrong. When Jesus saw how the Temple was turned into a worldly marketplace, he threw out the money-changers and the vendors (cf. Matthew 21:12–13).

We have to learn to be patient also with ourselves. "Have patience with all things, but chiefly have patience with yourself. Do not lose courage in considering your own imperfections, but instantly set about remedying them—every day begin the task anew" (St. Francis de Sales).

18
Going All the Way

Dashrath Manjhi was a poor laborer in a village in Bihar, India. At a young age, he had run away from home. But later he returned to his village, got married, and found a job. His wife would regularly bring him lunch, crossing the Gehlour hills. But one day, she slipped and was seriously injured. This eventually led to her death.

Manjhi was distressed, but the loss of his wife led him to decide to carve a passage through the Gehlour hills so that his village could have easier access to medical attention. People thought he was crazy.

From 1960 to 1983, using only a hammer and chisel, he carved a road 110 m long, 9.1 m wide and 7.6 m deep through the hillock. After 22 years of work, Dashrath shortened the distance between the two sides of the hill from 55 km to 15 km. "Though most villagers taunted me at first," Manjhi recalled, "there were quite a few who lent me support later by giving me food and helping me buy my tools." People called him the Mountain Man.

Manjhi died of gall bladder cancer on August 17, 2007 at the age of 73. In recognition of his service, the Government of Bihar gave him a state funeral.

Manjhi personifies many of the virtues we have previously seen: fortitude, magnanimity, generosity, patience. And one more: perseverance.

Perseverance is about finishing what we have begun. It is about going all the way.

"Many people begin, but few finish. And we, who are trying to behave as God's children, have to be among those few. Remember that only work that is well done and lovingly completed deserves the praise of the Lord which is to be found in Holy Scripture: 'better is the end of a task than its beginning' (Ecclesiastes 7:8)" (St. Josemaría, "Working for God").

Pope Francis has said that we live in what he calls the "culture of the ephemeral" or "culture of the provisional." People don't want to commit themselves to a lifetime task, they want to be able to jump ship when the going gets rough. But in this way, they will not be able to accomplish anything. If today I want to be an engineer, tomorrow a doctor, the day after a lawyer, I will end up being a beggar. If I go on a trip, and I keep changing my mind about where I want to go, I will end up nowhere.

But perseverance is needed not only for earthly success. Jesus himself tells us that "he who endures to the end will be saved" (Matthew 24:13). Our own eternal happiness depends on it. You and I are called to be holy, and this requires that we be persistent in our struggle to be more Christlike each single day. If we fail, we can start again, with God's grace. That's why Jesus gave us confession, where we can go "seventy-times seven" (Matthew 18:22) for forgiveness. St. Josemaría said that trying to be holy means just this: "beginning and beginning again, always just beginning."

Whatever path we have chosen in order to give ourselves to God, whether it be in marriage or in celibacy, we need to renew our love each day. And where do we renew it? In the sacraments and in prayer. For it is the Lord who renews us.

"Have you not known? Have you not heard? The LORD is the everlasting God, the Creator of the ends of the earth. He does not faint or grow weary, his understanding is unsearchable. He gives power to the faint, and to him who has no might he increases strength. Even youths shall faint and be weary, and young men shall fall exhausted; but they who wait for the LORD shall renew their strength, they shall mount up with wings like eagles, they shall run and not be weary, they shall walk and not faint" (Isaiah 40:28–31).

19
Surpass Yourself

Charles Michael Schwab (1862 –1939) was an American steel magnate who grew Bethlehem Steel into the second largest steel company in the world.

In his book *Succeeding with What You Have*, he tells the story of how he had once a factory where the mill manager seemed unable to inspire his men to do their best. The manager told Schwab that he had tried all sorts of ways: coaxing, pushing, swearing…but to no avail.

As they were speaking, it happened that the day shift was about to leave, and the night shift would come on duty. Schwab asked a workman for a piece of chalk. Then he asked the workman, "How many batches of steel has your shift made today?"

"Six," he replied.

Schwab wrote a big number "6" on the floor and then left. When the night shift came in they saw the "6" and asked about it.

"The big boss was in here today," said the day men. "He asked us how many heats we had made, and we told him six. He chalked it down."

The next morning, Schwab passed through the same mill. He saw that someone from the night shift had erased the "6" and written "7" in its place. He went back at night and the "7" had been replaced by a "10." That mill eventually became the best performer.

"Citior, altior, fortior" —faster, higher, stronger: that's the Olympic motto. It's the attitude we need to have in life, whether it be in the personal, social, professional, or spiritual aspect. "Don't flutter around like a hen when you

can soar like an eagle" (St. Josemaría, *The Way*, no 7). Soaring like an eagle requires achieving little goals one at a time, surpassing oneself one step at a time.

Terry Laughlin, founder of *Total Immersion*, has taught hundreds of people how to swim freestyle—especially in open water—without exhausting oneself. One of his "students" is a 94-year-old doctor who has swam 500 meters without any problem. One of Terry's secrets is the idea of continuous improvement. He says that each time he steps into the water, he needs to know what he is trying to accomplish in that swim, what improvement he is trying to make.

Terry, who is over 65 years old, says, "After 38 years of swimming, coaching and teaching, after over 15 million meters of swimming (I average about 500,000 meters per year), I'm still making regular advances in my control, efficiency and ease. I also swim 1500 meters faster than I did as an 18-year-old college freshman in 1969."

A student may not be able to sit for three hours to study, but he could start off with 10-minute periods while taking 1-minute rests in between, until he finishes his work. A person with a sad or surly disposition could start trying for a time to smile at least once a day, then twice, then thrice.... Someone who wants to develop his Rosary devotion might perhaps want to start with 5 Hail Mary's a day, or 10, and build up from there for the next two months.

St. Josemaría said that we need to "grow in the face of obstacles!" (*The Way,* no. 12). When faced with challenges we can grow in wisdom, in courage, in faith, in love.... Problems are opportunities for growth. He adds, "God's grace will not fail you: *'Inter medium montium pertransibunt aquae!'* You shall pass through the mountains!" (*The Way,* no. 12). We should not forget the miracles that grace can work in our soul. Through prayer and frequent reception of the sacraments, grace can make us new, it can recreate us, it can help us surpass ourselves.

St. Gregory of Nyssa, in his *Vita Moysis,* wrote that "we are in a certain way our own parents, creating ourselves as we ourselves wish to be and, through our will, forming ourselves in accordance with the model that we choose." It's up to us to decide whether we want to grow or not.

"Therefore when we explain the reason for our spontaneous reactions, rather than saying 'that's the way I am,' we should often admit: 'that's the way I have made myself'" ("Authors of our Own Lives" in www.opusdei.org).

20
Catching God's Attention

When Cardinal Joseph Ratzinger (future Pope Benedict XVI) was Prefect of the Sacred Congregation for the Doctrine of Faith, he lived just outside St. Peter's Square. Since his office was on the other side of St. Peter's, he would cross it each day on foot to go to work, dressed in an ordinary black cassock. It would happen that as he crossed, some tourists would stop him. Not that they recognized him—they simply wanted to ask him to take their photo. And that is what he would do, gladly, not caring that the tourists had not recognized the head of one of the Vatican's most important departments. Upon his election, Benedict XVI said that he considered himself "a lowly worker in the Lord's vineyard."

The Gospels give us many examples of humility. We find one of them in St. Luke, where he tells us the story of Zacchaeus. The rich tax collector had been wanting to see Jesus, and when his chance came, he did something only children would do: he clambered up a tree to get a better view. And he caught Jesus' attention.

"Zacchaeus, make haste and come down; for I must stay at your house today" (Luke 19:5). I must! At other occasions, Jesus had said He must suffer, He must die, He must rise again. Now He **must** see Zacchaeus. And right away!

Lucky man! By scrambling up the sycamore tree, Zacchaeus knew he would make a fool of himself—it would be humiliating and ridiculous for a chief tax collector to do such a childish act. But that's how he made Jesus turned his head, that's how he created a situation where Jesus **must** do something for him. By going up the tree, he lowered himself in the eyes of men, he humbled himself, he exposed himself to humiliation. And his humility drew the gaze of Jesus.

What does it mean to be humble? To be humble means to be realistic: to know who and what I am, and to know who and what God is. *"Noverim me, noverim Te"* ("Let me know myself, let me know Thee"), St. Augustine prayed. It means letting the Holy Spirit search my heart with the light of truth and the fire of love.

Humility is realism. For some people, being realistic means looking only at the problems. But they fail to see that there's Someone bigger than the problems.

Humility is realism. It makes me **discover the good** that God has done for me, and to **confess the evil** I have done.

Zacchaeus' humility was genuine. It moved him to resolve to do two things: **share the goods** he had received, and to **repent and make up for the evil** he had committed. "Behold, Lord, the half of my goods I give to the poor; and if I have defrauded any one of anything, I restore it fourfold" (verse 8).

Humility leads us to give generously, because the gifts God has given us are given for a specific mission, a mission unique to each one. There are responsibilities attached to every God-given gift. "Every one to whom much is given, of him will much be required; and of him to whom men commit much they will demand the more" (Luke 12:48).

Humility leads me to regret the offenses I have committed against God and against others. It requires me to restore the honor, or respect, or peace, or joy, or material possessions I have unjustly taken from them. It moves me to repair the damage I have done, through works of love and service.

Pride makes us eager to catch the attention of men. Humility makes us capable of catching the attention of God.

21
In the Presence of the Great "Other"

On August 5, 1958, 38-year-old Father Karol Wojtyla (future John Paul II) received a letter from Cardinal Wyszynski, asking him to come immediately to the Cardinal's office in Warsaw.

When Father Karol arrived, Cardinal Wyszynski told him that the Pope (at that time Pius XII) had named him auxiliary bishop of Krakow.

Wojtyla accepted, then went right away to a convent of Ursuline nuns close by, asking the nuns if he could come in to pray.

They did not know him, but because he was

dressed in a cassock, they let him in and left him alone in the chapel.

Hours passed and when the nuns were taking supper, they thought of offering him something to eat. When they went to the chapel, Karol was prostrate on the floor in front of the tabernacle. They then asked if he wanted to have something to eat.

"My train doesn't leave for Krakow until after midnight. Please let me stay here. I have a lot to talk about with the Lord," he replied.

We have seen last week that humility is realism: knowing who God is and knowing who we are. Once we get a little idea of just how great God is, and how tiny we are, we understand right away why we cannot live life without God and that we always "have a lot to talk about with the Lord."

Hence, an immediate consequence of humility is a prayerful spirit. A humble man necessarily prays, and a very humble man prays all the time. But a proud man doesn't see the need for it.

By "prayerful spirit" we don't mean reciting prayers now and then. Prayer does not mean rattling on before God about our frustrations and disappointments, our needs and wants.

Prayer means living our entire day in an

attitude of **listening** to God's voice and **preparedness** to do His will: a humble man is **attentive** and **docile** to God's word.

Philip Yancey says, "Most of my struggles in the Christian life circle around the same two themes: why God doesn't act the way we want God to, and why I don't act the way God wants me to. Prayer is the precise point where those themes converge" (*Prayer: Does It Make Any Difference?*, p. 17).

Listening. What can we do to listen? "What are the sources of Christian prayer?" the *Compendium of the Catechism of the Catholic Church* asks.

And it replies, "They are: the **Word of God** which gives us 'the surpassing knowledge' of Christ (Philippians 3:8); the **Liturgy of the Church** that proclaims, makes present and communicates the mystery of salvation; the **theological virtues**; and **everyday situations** because in them we can encounter God" (*Compendium of the Catechism of the Catholic Church*, no. 558).

When we listen, we learn to see things from a very different angle: "Prayer is the act of seeing reality from God's point of view" (Philip Yancey, *Prayer: Does It Make Any Difference?*, p. 29). We discover that "the earth is full of the steadfast love of the LORD" (Psalm 33:5). We are moved to exclaim, "In wisdom you have made them all" (Psalm 104:24).

Preparedness. Listening makes us realize that God always acts for our good (cf. Romans 8:28) and the good of everyone. When we are assured of this, we find it logical and easy to say, "Thy will be done!"

Humility leads us to put aside our ambitions, our dreams, our personal projects in favor of a far greater Project. After all, our talents and gifts have been given for a purpose, for a mission which is unique to each one of us. But that mission that does not discard our dreams, and rather takes them to a higher level. It lifts us higher than we could ever have reached.

"And I heard the voice of the Lord saying, 'Whom shall I send, and who will go for us?' Then I said, 'Here am I! Send me'" (Isaiah 6:8).

22
Not to Be Served but to Serve

The following story was published by Pino Corrias of the Italian magazine *Vanity Fair* just a short time after Pope Francis was elected.

"A few mornings ago, coming out into the hallway, the Pope found outside his door the Swiss Guard standing with his halberd at attention.

"He asked: 'And what are you doing here? Have you been up all night?'

"'Yes,' replied the guard with deference.

"'On your feet?'

"'I took over from my colleague.'

"'Are you not tired?'

"'It's my duty Holiness, for your safety.'

"Pope Francis looked at him with a certain sweetness. He went back to his room and after a minute he came back out with a chair in hand: 'At least sit down and rest.'

"The guard crossed his eyes: 'Forgive me, but I cannot! The regulation does not allow that.'

"'The rules?'

"'My captain, Holiness.'

"'Oh, really? Well, I'm the Pope and I ask you to sit down.'

"So between the regulation and the Pope, the Swiss Guard chose the chair. He also accepted the jam sandwich that the Pope personally brought him with his Argentinian smile. Before he could say anything, the Holy Father wished him a good bite: *'Bon appetit* brother.'"

Jesus said, "The Son of man came not to be served but to serve" (Matthew 20:28), and He instructed His followers: "Learn from me; for I am gentle and lowly in heart" (Matthew 11:29).

The "lowly in heart" seek to serve, and do not expect to be served.

Humility necessarily brings with it not only the spirit of prayer (as we saw last time) but also the spirit of service. A man striving to be humble prays and serves as well. (I said, "striving to be humble" because as long as we are on earth, we can never conclusively boast, "Oh, thank God I'm humble!")

A man striving to be humble thinks little of himself and puts his mind, heart, and soul in God and in others.

A humble person quickly detects opportunities to serve. He does not wait to be asked. Our Lady, model of humility, realized that the wine in Cana was running out and did something about it.

True service does not discriminate. In the Last Supper, even if Jesus knew that Judas would betray him and Peter would deny him, he washed their feet just the same.

True service born out of love does not require a receipt, a recognition of the service done. After Jesus had turned the water to wine, our Lady didn't go around announcing the miracle and how she helped to make it happen.

True service does not call attention to itself, does not seek approval or applause. It does not make a fuss of the favor it has rendered. It only aims to give glory to God: "He must increase, I must decrease" (John 3:30).

True service is a characteristic of great leaders, whose aim is not to make themselves great before men but to lead their men to greatness.

Msgr. Vincent Tran Ngoc Thu, one of St. John Paul II's secretaries, said that the Pope could reach for the telephone and call any of his secretaries if he ever needed anything. But he hardly used it. If he needed something, he would go to the office of the person concerned.

The cardinals who elected Benedict XVI remarked how moved they were by his self-effacing service during the meetings before the papal conclave. The cardinals were divided into language groups and the future Benedict XVI happened to be the Dean of Cardinals and had to preside over the meetings. When he spoke to one group, he would talk to them in their language. No wonder the cardinals realized he would make an ideal Shepherd for the whole Church. For whoever knows how to serve knows how to lead.

23
Humiliation Can Be Good for You

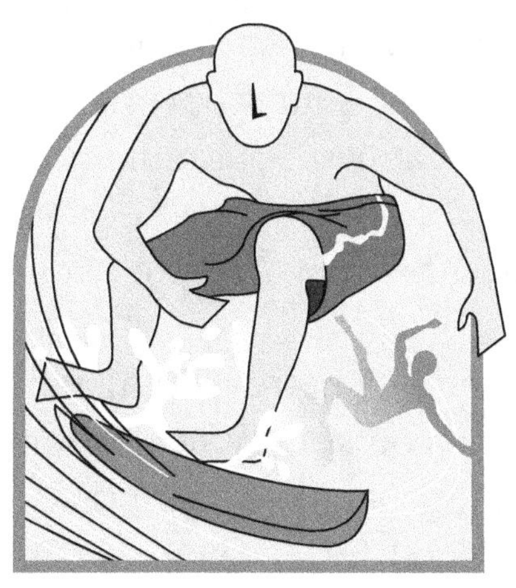

On February 21, 1957, Professor Joseph Ratzinger had to present himself for his public habilitation lecture which, together with the post-doctoral thesis, would make him eligible to teach. He was very nervous because the second examiner, a well-known theologian named Michael Schmaus, was not in his favor. Ratzinger's position was so contentious that during his defense in the lecture hall, a heated debate between his supervisor, Gottlieb Söhngen, and Professor Schmaus ensued.

"It was an extraordinary situation," remarked Ratzinger, now Pope Emeritus Benedict, while speaking to Peter Seewald in the recently released book *Last Testament: In His Own Words*.

Four years earlier, in 1953, after he had just earned his doctorate, the Rector of the university had told Ratzinger that "he hoped he would see me as a colleague in the seminary," reminisced Pope Benedict. That gave his ego a boost.

But the battle for the post-doctorate thesis was a great humiliation for him. "I was made very small on this occasion," Pope Benedict commented. "That does someone good: to recognize once again, yes, one's utter poverty and to stand there not like a great hero, but rather as a lowly candidate."

From that experience, he drew a lesson: "one needs humiliations."

He further explained, "I believe that it is dangerous for a young person simply to go from achieving goal after goal, generally being praised along the way. So it is good for a young person to experience his limit, occasionally to be dealt with critically, to suffer his way through a period of negativity, to recognize his own limits himself, not simply to win victory after victory. A human being needs to endure something in order to learn to assess himself correctly, and not least to learn to think with others. Then he will not simply judge others hastily and stay aloof, but rather accept them positively, in his labours and his weaknesses."

One needs humiliations. Indeed, humiliations are a path to humility.

Humiliations may come from other people, by way of truths told to our face, or by way of lies. The Pharisees rejected Jesus because he ate and drank "with tax collectors and sinners" (Matthew 9:11, Mark 2:15, Luke 5:30) and entertained women of low repute (cf. Luke 7:36–40, John 4:3–42, 8:1–11). They falsely accused him of casting out demons by the power of Beelzebul (cf. Matthew 12:24, Luke 11:15).

We may also be humiliated by certain situations or circumstances, when we see our helplessness before some problems.

We are humiliated by failure, but failure is a good remedy for pride.

"At times I have surprised myself," says Pope Francis, "by thinking that a few very rigid people would do well to slip a little, so that they could remember that they are sinners and thus meet Jesus. I think back to the words of God's servant John Paul I, who during a Wednesday audience said, 'The Lord loves humility so much that sometimes he permits serious sins. Why? In order that those who committed these sins may, after repenting, remain humble'" (*The Name of God is Mercy*).

24
Inner Peace: Fruit of Humility

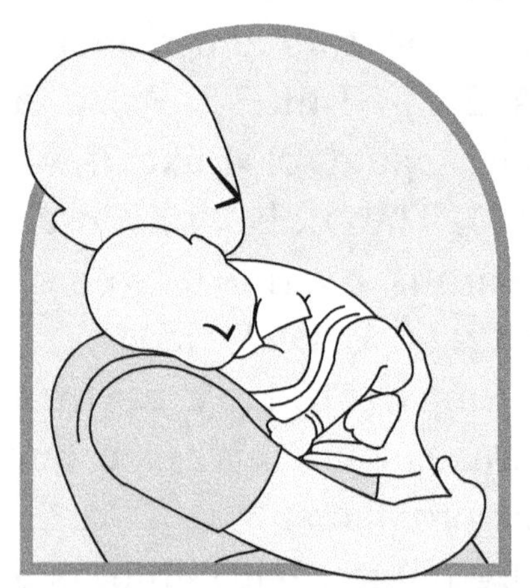

Blessed Alvaro del Portillo was regarded by all who knew him as the epitome of serenity. A story from his youth illustrates it.

When he was still an engineering student, his youngest brother Carlos accidentally knocked over a bottle of ink on some drawings which Alvaro had been working on. Carlos was naturally apprehensive about how his brother might react.

To his surprise, however, when Alvaro got home, he sat Carlos on his knee and explained to him calmly how important the project was, and gently advised him to be more careful next time. That was all!

One of the consequences of humility is deep inner peace and serenity. Why is this?

The explanation is quite straightforward. Humility makes us know our littleness, and it shows God's greatness. It makes us realize that we are children and leads us to place ourselves in the hands of our Father God. St. Teresa of Avila says *"quien a Dios tiene nada le falta – sólo Dios basta"* (whoever has God lacks nothing else: God alone suffices).

The person who accepts his littleness is like a baby who sleeps safe and secure in his mother's arms. "I have calmed and quieted my soul, like a child quieted at its mother's breast; like a child that is quieted is my soul" (Psalm 131:2).

Does that mean that we renounce all responsibility? By no means. We want to be children: responsible children. So we will do our utmost to fulfill our duties, but we will leave God to decide on the results.

On the other hand, pride, which blinds us from the truth, leads us to think that we need to be always in control. It makes us believe that everyone, including God, should follow what we say. That, of course, is a great delusion.

Pride makes us worried and fearful, uselessly spending our energy on things beyond our control.

Pride makes us upset when things don't turn out the way we want them.

Pride generates anxiety, it generates anger.

But humility generates peace.

A person striving to be humble is like the deep water: even as a storm rages on the surface, calm reigns in the depths.

Humility reminds a person that he is an instrument in God's hands. His role is to make himself available whenever and wherever God needs him, as long as God needs him, and lets God take care of the results.

During the Protestant revolt in the sixteenth century, St. Francis de Sales, a patient and peaceful man, decided to go to Switzerland, where everyone had turned Calvinist, to try to bring them back to the Faith.

No one was convinced. They thought he was crazy. Only his cousin accompanied him in his expedition. His father thought he was mad and refused to give him any help. The diocese was too poor to support him.

For three years, he trudged through the countryside. People slammed the door in his face and threw rocks at him. In the bitter winters, his feet froze so badly that they bled as he tramped through the snow. He had no place to sleep, but once he slept in a tree to avoid wolves. He tied himself to a branch to keep from falling out and was so frozen the next morning he had to be cut down. And after three years, his cousin had left him alone and he had not made one convert. But he kept his peace.

Since no one would even open their door, he wrote out his sermons, copied them by hand, and slipped them under the doors. Talk about door-to-door marketing! Since the adults did not want to listen, he talked to children.

The result? When he returned home, he had converted 40,000 people back to Catholicism.

25
On Not Taking Oneself too Seriously

It was one of those Wednesday audiences at Castelgandolfo during his first year as Pope in 2005. Benedict XVI was about to leave for the World Youth Day in Cologne and was addressing the crowd who cheered him again and again. After greeting them in several languages and inviting them to come to the World Youth Day, he waved goodbye and turned around.

In a few seconds he was back, chuckling and admitted, "I forgot to greet the Italians!" And the crowd laughed with him.

After greeting the Italians, he waved again, and disappeared. But only for a few seconds. He was back, more amused than ever.

"I forgot the most important thing! I forgot to give you the blessing!" More laughter.

"Now and then," Pope Benedict once said in an interview, "God gives you a nudge and says,

'Don't take yourself too seriously!'"

Pride makes a person think he is like God (cf. Genesis 3:5) and since one does not joke around with God, a proud person hates being laughed at or ridiculed. "The pagan always strives to be self-contained, self-sufficient, self-satisfied, self-obsessed. The saint finds all sufficiency in Christ alone, and cares nothing for self. There is no surer path to damnation than taking oneself too seriously" (Francis Randolph, *Wisdom at Play*).

St. Teresa of Avila prayed, "Deliver us, Lord, from sour-faced saints!"

John XXIII once visited a hospital in Rome called the Hospital of the Holy Spirit. Shortly after entering the building, he was introduced to the sister who ran the hospital.

"Holy Father," she said, "I am the superior of the Holy Spirit."

"You're very lucky," said the Pope. "I'm only the Vicar of Christ!"

In one of her writings where she speaks at length about prayer, St. Teresa of Avila ends by saying, "It seems to me I have explained this matter, but perhaps I've made it clear only to myself."

As Pope John Paul II's Parkinson's disease progressed, journalists would often ask him how he felt. On one occasion, he replied, "From the neck up, not bad!" On another, he said, "I don't really know. I have not read the newspapers." (He was referring to the fact that the newspapers were always speculating about his health.)

Even from the human point of view, a sense of humor is so important. "You don't stop laughing because you grow old. You grow old because you stop laughing" (Michael Pritchard). Studies seem to show that laughter is good for one's health.

Some may object and say that the Gospels never speak about Jesus smiling or laughing. But Father Joseph Soria, in his book about St. Josemaría (*Maestro de Buen Humor,* "Teacher of good humor") gives a reasonable explanation: Jesus indeed was smiling all the time, but if the Gospels were to record the fact, they would have to repeat many times, "And Jesus smiled and said…"

If Jesus was always serious and solemn, children would not have liked getting close to him (cf. Matthew 19:14, Mark 10:14, Luke 18:16). But they did.

When he spoke to the Roman Curia a couple of days before Christmas in 2014, Pope Francis reminded everyone, "A bit of good humor is very good for us! It will do us much good to pray St. Thomas More's prayer frequently: I pray it every day, and it helps me."

So let us all pray with the Holy Father:

"Grant me, O Lord, good digestion, and also something to digest.

"Grant me a healthy body, and the necessary good humor to maintain it.

"Grant me a simple soul that knows to treasure all that is good and that doesn't frighten easily at the sight of evil, but rather finds the means to put things back in their place.

"Give me a soul that knows not boredom, grumblings, sighs and laments, nor excess of stress, because of that obstructing thing called 'I.'

"Grant me, O Lord, a sense of good humor.

"Allow me the grace to be able to take a joke to discover in life a bit of joy, and to be able to share it with others."

26
Choosing Joy

In her lifetime, Mother Teresa received many visitors who wanted to know more about her work and the secret of her "success."

One time she received a group of professors from the United States. She brought them around the house where they took care of the dying. At the end of the visit, one of them asked Mother Teresa, "Mother, would you have any advice for us?"

"Yes," she replied, "smile at each other."

"Rejoice always" (I Thessalonians 5:16–17), St. Paul commands.

Why should we rejoice always? What is the root of joy?

Christian joy is not "the happiness of a healthy animal" (St. Josemaría, *The Way*, no. 659). The Christian is joyful not because things always turn out right for him, that events always meet his expectations.

Christian joy does not come from having many things. "Technological society has succeeded in multiplying the opportunities for pleasure, but it has great difficulty in generating joy" (Paul VI, *Gaudete in Domino*).

Christian joy does not come from the world outside. It comes from the inside. "Let the hearts of those who seek the Lord rejoice" (Psalms 105:3).

Christian joy is a sharing in the joy of Jesus, who wants His joy to be ours and who wants that our "joy be made full" (cf. John 15:11).

From where does Jesus draw His joy?

"If Jesus radiates such peace, such assurance, such happiness, such availability," Blessed Pope Paul VI explains, "it is by reason of the inexpressible love by which He knows that He is loved by His Father" (*Gaudete in Domino*).

Christian joy comes from the awareness that we are children of a **Father** who is infinite Wisdom, Goodness, and Power himself. Nothing on earth can beat a Dad with those credentials.

Christian joy comes from finding **Jesus**: "The disciples saw the Lord, and were glad" (John 20:20).

Christian joy, together with charity and peace are among the fruits of the **Holy Spirit** (cf. Galatians 5:22), who bears witness "that we are children of God" (Romans 8:16).

Christian joy breaks out when one who has sinned repents, confesses his sins, and receives the priest's absolution. "Every absolution is, in a certain way, a jubilee of the heart, which brings joy not only the faithful and the Church, but first of all to God Himself" (Pope Francis, March 4, 2016).

But what about sorrow and sadness?

St. Paul says there are two kinds of sorrow: "The sorrow, that is according to God works penance steadfast unto salvation, but the sorrow of the world works death" (II Corinthians 7:10). The sorrow according to God is the sorrow of repentance. The sorrow of the world results from pride, envy, greed, ambition, lust, laziness. "You are unhappy? — Think: there must be an obstacle between God and me. You will seldom be wrong" (St. Josemaría, *The Way,* no. 662).

And yes, we are saddened when we do not have the basic things that we need, when we see suffering and injustice around us. However, we should never forget that "God never ruffles the joy of his children, except to prepare them for a certain, far greater joy" (Alessandro Manzoni). In God's plan, pain has a purpose. What does that mean? Look at the Crucified Jesus and let Him explain.

"If things go well, let us rejoice, blessing God who makes them prosper. And if they go badly? Let us rejoice, blessing God who allows us to share in the sweetness of his Cross" (St. Josemaría, *The Way*, no. 658)

Jesus sends all of us out to our families and friends and colleagues: "Go home to your friends, and tell them how much the Lord has done for you, and how he has had mercy on you" (Mark 5:19). We need to tell them, "Come and hear, all you who fear God, and I will tell what he has done for me" (Psalm 66:16).

The Gospel means "good news." If it is really good news that we bring, there is no reason to wear long faces. "The children of God should always be sowers of peace and joy" (St. Josemaría Escrivá, *Furrow*, no. 59).

27
The Conversation that Never Happened

"Mary, wake up!"

"Huh? What? Do you know what time it is?"

"I know. But we have to get out of here."

"What did you say?"

"We have to get out of here. Herod wants to kill our Baby!"

"Where on earth did you get that news?"

"Well, an angel told me."

"When?"

"As I dreamt."

"Ah, Joseph, you can't believe in dreams all the time. Besides, if it is that important, the angel would have told me as well! Now get back to sleep and let's talk about it tomorrow."

Imagine what would have happened if this conversation really took place: there would be no Messiah, no Christmas, no Church, no Sacraments, no salvation, no future for you and me, no meaning to life, and nothing to make life worth living.

"Many great things depend — don't forget it — on whether you and I live our lives as God wants" (St. Josemaría, *The Way*, no. 755).

St. Paul explains: "For as by one man's disobedience many were made sinners, so by one man's obedience many will be made righteous" (Romans 5:19). What a great difference the disobedience or obedience of just one man makes!

Obedience is one immediate consequence of humility. Jesus showed us the way: "he humbled himself and became obedient unto death, even death on a cross" (Philippians 2:8).

When God called Abraham, he (Abraham) was already 75 years old (cf. Genesis 12:13), ready for retirement. Yet he obeyed God's call, waiting till he was 100 years old (25 years!) for God to fulfill his promise of giving him a son (cf. Genesis 21:5).

Abraham obeyed, Moses obeyed, Joshua obeyed, Samuel obeyed...Mary obeyed, Joseph obeyed, Jesus obeyed, Peter obeyed.... Everyone who has become a main character in the History of Salvation had to obey. You and I are also called to become characters in that History. You and I are also called to obedience.

One difficulty with obedience is that God's will at times tends to clash with ours. The angel had told Joseph, "Rise, take the child and his mother, and flee to Egypt, and remain there till I tell you; for Herod is about to search for the child, to destroy him" (Matthew 2:13).

We don't like sudden changes of plans, do we? And St. Joseph had to face that, too. Moreover, he could have thought, "What poor planning! And I thought God knew everything!" But he obeyed just the same.

Sometimes the difficulty lies in the fact that God does not always specify the details. The angel's instructions were to stay in Egypt "till I tell you" (Matthew 2:13). "Till I tell you" is not very clear, is it? Joseph could have asked for more details: "Does that mean one week, one month, one year...?" But those were the only instructions, and he obeyed.

Another difficulty with obedience is that God does not always contact us directly. He often speaks through a middleman. Samuel knew God's will through Eli (cf. I Samuel 3), Saul got to know about it through Ananias (cf. Acts 9). And it can also happen that the middleman is not easy to get along with.

At times He speaks through the circumstances we find ourselves in. Therese of Lisieux had dreams of being a martyr. But there was no way she could be a martyr in the convent. By meditating on chapter 13 of St. Paul's First Letter to the Corinthians, she concluded that God simply wanted her to be love, that is, to personify charity in her dealings with the other sisters.

Every miracle in the History of Salvation is a story of obedience. Miracles happen when, with full trust in God's Wisdom, Goodness, and Power, we pray, "Thy will be done."

28
He Puts You at Ease

On his deathbed, King Charles II of England apologized to the people accompanying him in his last moments, "You must pardon me, gentlemen, for being a most unconscionable time a-dying." Father George W. Rutler recalled these words of King Charles in his essay "Christ the Gentleman."

They came to my mind upon reading what Msgr. Fernando Ocáriz (Auxiliary Vicar of Opus Dei) said in his homily for the funeral of the Prelate of Opus Dei Bishop Javier Echevarría on December 15, 2016, "The day before he died, he [Bishop Echevarría] told me he was worried that he was being a nuisance to the persons who were taking care of him."

Father Rutler also quotes King Charles II who defines a gentleman as "one who puts those around him at ease." His words made me think again of Bishop Echevarría. Whether it be in a meeting or over a meal, he always made one feel at ease. He was not one to impress others with his authority or knowledge.

A man who puts us at ease is one who does not give himself too much importance, who does not need to show himself as superior. He knows that his talents are not for him to brag about, but are given to him to serve God and his fellow creatures.

Our Lord Jesus Christ, "meek and humble of heart" (Matthew 11:29), put his disciples at ease. In the Last Supper, He knew his death was approaching and so "he began to be sorrowful and troubled" and told His apostles "My soul is very sorrowful, even to death" (Matthew 26:37–38). Yet he did not talk more about His sorrow, did not ask His Apostles for promises to be faithful, but rather encouraged them: "Let not your hearts be troubled" (John 14:1).

Jesus put His disciples at ease. That's why they didn't hesitate to ask Him questions: "Who is the greatest?" (cf. Matthew 23:11), "Will only a few be saved?" (Luke 13:23), "Explain the parable" (Matthew 15:15). The apostles didn't fear being judged by Him, or rejected, or snobbed, or put down.

In His presence, we don't have to pretend to be anything. With His gentleness, He tells us, "Just be yourself!"

Our Lord Jesus Christ, "meek and humble of heart," came as a Child, as a humble Carpenter. He disguised Himself as a criminal, and now He disguises Himself as Bread. Just so that you and I will show ourselves as we are before Him, with both our virtues and vices, with our good deeds and our sins. In that way, He can easily cleanse us and forgive us, especially in the Sacrament of Confession.

The saints learned from Jesus how to be meek and humble of heart, and how to put others at ease.

Stanislaw Grygiel, a Polish philosopher and friend of St. John Paul II, narrates that when the latter was still Archbishop, he once went to a small parish for a visit. He arrived a bit earlier than scheduled and started to walk around a bit. He poked his head into a classroom. The parish priest was teaching catechism to some children.

"Do you know why I have come?" he asked the children.

"Yes, I know," one seven-year-old boy replied. "You came to learn something."

"Yes, you're right!"

And with that, he sat beside the boy and stayed there until the end of the lesson.

The man who strives to be humble learns how to put those around him at ease. He learns the humility of Jesus the Gentleman: Perfect God, Perfect Man.

29
"Slow to Anger"
(Psalm 103:8)

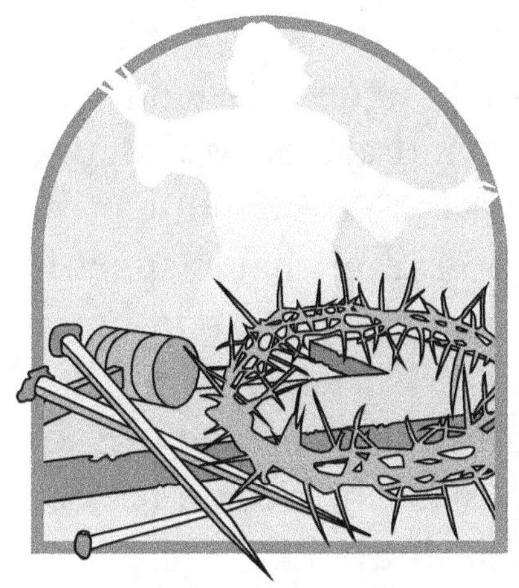

Cardinal John Tong, in his book *Challenges and Hopes: Stories from the Catholic Church in China*, tells the story of a priest who, before the communist takeover, had a parish of 200 Catholics.

"Some time after 1949," the Cardinal writes, "he could no longer function as a priest. Instead he was assigned to carry charcoal. That was hard work for an educated man unaccustomed to heavy manual labor."

Initially, he did not understand why God should let such a thing happen to him. But instead of letting himself be overcome by anger and self-pity, he decided to do his job meekly.

"In the 1980s, he was finally allowed to return to his church and to resume his sacramental ministry," the Cardinal continued, "but he could only preach and pray on church property. Yet

800 people now crowd into that church every weekend...."

Jesus taught: "Blessed are the meek, for they shall inherit the earth" (Matthew 5:5). Meekness helps us moderate and channel our anger. Meekness helps us to win hearts.

Father Salvador Canals writes, "We all tend to think that it is better and easier to do good by being noisy and bossy; that people can be taught by threats and pressure; that respect is obtained just by raising one's voice and being authoritarian" ("Meekness," in *Jesus as Friend*).

The Lord Jesus, however, in teaching or correcting his disciples, "will not break a bruised reed or quench a smoldering wick" (Matthew 12:20, quoting Isaiah 42:3). Instead, he treats them as friends (cf. John 15:15).

St. Josemaría teaches that "the Good Shepherd need not terrorize the sheep" (*Furrow*, no. 404). He taught that Christian apostolate is built on friendship and trust.

Even when we have to correct an erring person, we need to be gentle and kind, we need to moderate our impatience. "How often experience has taught us," Father Canals says, "that corrections and reproaches, made without human meekness, have closed the heart of the person who should have received them. This should help us remember that, when we cease to be a father, brother or friend to our neighbor, every word that leaves our lips carries the fatal germ of sterility."

The Good News can only spread through friendship and trust. "My friend, you feel on your shoulders and in your heart responsibility for other souls, the weight of other lives: never forget that trust cannot be imposed; it must be inspired. And without the trust of the people around you, who work with you and serve you, how bitter your life will be and how fruitless your mission" (*Jesus as Friend*).

How often we would like that God will swiftly correct misbehavior, invoking fire and brimstone from heaven to strike the evildoer. But our Lord says that that is not His way (cf. Luke 9:55). "Your ill-temper, your roughness, your rigidity (not very Christian!) are why you find yourself alone, in the loneliness of someone who is selfish, embittered, eternally discontented or resentful; and they are also why you are surrounded not by love but by indifference, coldness, resentment and lack of trust" (*Jesus as Friend*).

What is the fruit of meekness? "When you have in your hands the hearts of people whom you wish to improve, if you are able to attract them through the meekness of Christ, you have already gone halfway on your apostolic road. When they love you and trust you, when they are content, the field is ready for sowing. For their hearts are like fertile ground, ready to receive the white grain of your word as an apostle or educator. If you know how to speak without wounding, although you may have to correct or reprimand, hearts will not close themselves to you. The seed will fall on truly fertile ground and the harvest will be plentiful" (*Jesus as Friend*).

O Jesus, meek and humble of heart, make our hearts like unto yours!

30
"They Shall See God"
(Matthew 5:8)

Early last year, the following story made the rounds in cyberspace.

A girl bought an iPad. When her father saw it, he asked her "What was the first thing you did when you bought it?"

"I put an anti-scratch sticker on the screen and bought a cover for the iPad," she replied.

"Did someone force you to do so?"

"No."

"Don't you think it's an insult to the manufacturer?"

"No Dad! In fact, they even recommend using a cover for the iPad."

"Did you cover it because it was cheap and ugly?"

"Actually, I covered it because I didn't want it to get damage and decrease in value."

"When you put the cover on, didn't it reduce

the iPad's beauty?"

"I think it looks better and it is worth it for the protection it gives my iPad."

The father looked lovingly at his daughter and said, "Yet if I had asked you to cover your body which is much more precious than the iPad, would you have readily agreed?"

She was speechless.

Modesty and purity are not the most important virtues, but we need them. The Lord says purity of heart is required to see God (cf. Matthew 5:8).

The power to generate new life is an awesome and sacred power. Awesome because a man and a woman become co-creators with God. Sacred because God is involved in every act of generation: for every baby conceived, God creates a soul. God operates through man's sexuality.

To misuse something sacred for other purposes must greatly offend God. The only occasion recorded where Jesus used violence is when He threw the vendors and money changers from the temple. That's what our bodies are— temples, sacred places. "Do you not know that your body is a temple of the Holy Spirit within you, which you have from God? You are not your own; you were bought with a price. So glorify

God in your body" (I Corinthians 6:19–20).

Moreover, a man or woman is not "something"—an object—to be used for the sake of obtaining pleasure, but "someone" to be loved for his/her own sake.

Our Lord taught, "You have heard that it was said, 'You shall not commit adultery.' But I say to you that every one who looks at a woman lustfully has already committed adultery with her in his heart."

He added, "If your right eye causes you to sin, pluck it out and throw it away; it is better that you lose one of your members than that your whole body be thrown into hell" (Matthew 5:27–29).

Perhaps we will then understand what Pope Francis told the Argentinian daily *La Voz del Pueblo:* "I have not watched TV since 1990. It's a promise that I made the Virgin of Carmen on the night of July 15, 1990. I told myself, 'It's not for me'."

As for football, he added, "I watch nothing. There is a Swiss Guard that every week tells me the results and how we are doing in the league table."

On one occasion, as he was delivering his Wednesday audience message, Pope Francis looked up from his prepared speech, and said,

"Would you mind if I tell you something personal? Do you know what I do before I go to bed? I tell the Lord, 'Lord, if you will, you can make me clean' (Matthew 8:2; Mark 1:40; Luke 5:12). Then I say five Our Fathers in honor of the Lord's Five Wounds."

Do I want to be made clean? Let me then ask the Lord in prayer, in Confession, in the Eucharist: "Lord, if You will, You can make me clean!"